The Giant Book
of Real Facts

by
Jake Jacobs

* * * * *

Published by Jake Jacobs

The Giant Book of Real Facts
Copyright© 2023 by Jake Jacobs

1.

The John Trumbull Birthplace is located in Lebanon, Connecticut, and is the birthplace of American artist John Trumbull.

2.

John Trumbull was born in the house on June 6, 1756.

3.

The house was built in 1720 by John's father, Jonathan Trumbull Sr., who later became the Governor of Connecticut and served during the American Revolutionary War.

4.

John Trumbull was an accomplished painter known for his historical and portrait paintings, many of which depict scenes from the American Revolutionary War.

5.

The birthplace is a Colonial-style house with a saltbox roof, a common architectural style of the time.

6.

The house has been preserved and restored to reflect its appearance during the 18th century.

7.

It was declared a National Historic Landmark in 1965.

8.

The birthplace is also listed on the National Register of Historic Places.

9.

The house is part of the Lebanon Historical Society and is open to the public as a museum.

10.

Visitors to the birthplace can explore the rooms and view exhibits related to John Trumbull's life and works.

11.

The house features period furnishings, artifacts, and displays that offer insight into daily life during the colonial era.

12.

John Trumbull had a passion for art from a young age and showed early talent as an artist.

13.

He pursued formal art education in London, where he studied under the renowned American artist Benjamin West.

14.

Trumbull's famous historical paintings include "The Declaration of Independence," "The Surrender of General Burgoyne," and "The Surrender of Lord Cornwallis."

15.

The artist aimed to accurately portray historical events and figures, earning him the nickname "The Painter of the Revolution."

16.

Trumbull's works are often seen as important visual records of early American history.

17.

The John Trumbull Birthplace offers guided tours to educate visitors about John Trumbull's life and artistry.

18.

The house is set in a scenic location in Lebanon, surrounded by picturesque landscapes and historic sites.

19.

The birthplace provides insights into the upbringing and influences that shaped John Trumbull's artistic career.

20.

John Trumbull's commitment to documenting American history through art helped preserve significant moments for future generations.

21.

Trumbull's artistry contributed to shaping the visual representation of the early United States.

22.

The birthplace's preservation showcases the importance of preserving cultural heritage and historical landmarks.

23.

The house reflects the architectural style and lifestyle of colonial New England.

24.

John Trumbull's dedication to portraying historical accuracy in his works contributed to their enduring impact.

25.

Trumbull's paintings are displayed in prominent institutions, including the United States Capitol Rotunda.

26.

The birthplace serves as a tribute to John Trumbull's legacy as an artist and his contributions to American art history.

27.

Visitors can gain insights into Trumbull's artistic techniques, inspirations, and the challenges he faced during his career.

28.

Trumbull's art often conveys the ideals of the American Revolution, patriotism, and the struggle for freedom.

29.

The birthplace's exhibits highlight Trumbull's collaborations with other notable figures of his time.

30.

Trumbull's depictions of key historical figures, such as George Washington and Thomas Jefferson, remain iconic.

31.

The birthplace provides a glimpse into the life of a prominent American family during the colonial era.

32.

The house's preservation efforts demonstrate the value of maintaining historical structures for educational purposes.

33.

Trumbull's dedication to historical accuracy required extensive research and attention to detail.

34.

The birthplace's location in Lebanon aligns with its historical significance as a colonial settlement.

35.

Trumbull's works continue to inspire artists, historians, and those interested in American history.

36.

The birthplace's architecture reflects the craftsmanship of early New England builders.

37.

Trumbull's efforts to capture the spirit of the American Revolution in his paintings earned him admiration and recognition.

38.

The birthplace's exhibits explore the broader context of American history and events that influenced Trumbull's art.

39.

Trumbull's portrayal of pivotal moments, such as the signing of the Declaration of Independence, remains iconic.

40.

The birthplace serves as a place of reflection on the contributions of American artists to the nation's cultural heritage.

41.

Trumbull's artistic style evolved over time, reflecting changing artistic trends and his own growth as an artist.

42.

The birthplace offers a window into the upbringing and family dynamics that shaped John Trumbull's worldview.

43.

Trumbull's dedication to documenting historical events contributed to the public's understanding of the nation's founding.

44.

The birthplace's preservation is a testament to the importance of commemorating significant figures in American history.

45.

Trumbull's artworks continue to be studied for their portrayal of historical figures' personalities and emotions.

46.

The birthplace's exhibits may include reproductions of Trumbull's works, providing visitors with an appreciation for his artistry.

47.

Trumbull's legacy extends beyond his paintings to his influence on American visual culture.

48.

The birthplace's educational programs and events contribute to fostering an appreciation for art and history.

49.

Trumbull's portraits often captured the unique qualities and strengths of his subjects.

50.

The John Trumbull Birthplace serves as a valuable resource for connecting present-day audiences with the artist's legacy and the historical events he depicted.

51.

The Mark Twain Home, also known as the Mark Twain House & Museum, is located at 351 Farmington Avenue in Hartford, Connecticut.

52.

The house was the residence of renowned American author Mark Twain, whose real name was Samuel Langhorne Clemens, and his family.

53.

The home was designed by architect Edward Tuckerman Potter and built in the High Gothic style, featuring ornate and distinctive architectural elements.

54.

Construction of the house began in 1873 and was completed in 1874.

55.

The Clemens family moved into the home in September 1874.

56.

The Mark Twain House was Mark Twain's primary residence from 1874 to 1891.

57.

The house was a place of creativity and inspiration for Twain, where he wrote some of his most famous works, including "The Adventures of Tom Sawyer" and "Adventures of Huckleberry Finn."

58.

The home's design and furnishings reflected the Victorian aesthetic of the time, with intricate details and luxurious materials.

59.

The house has 19 rooms, including the family's living quarters, servants' quarters, and Twain's study.

60.

The house features unique architectural elements, such as the ornate woodwork, decorative carvings, and stained glass windows.

61.

The dining room is adorned with a stunning mahogany table that can seat up to 22 people.

62.

The billiard room was a popular gathering spot for Twain and his friends.

63.

The house is known for its distinctive octagonal bay windows, which provide ample natural light.

64.

Twain's study, located on the second floor, was his private writing sanctuary where he penned many of his famous works.

65.

Twain's daughter, Susy Clemens, also had her own writing desk in the study, reflecting the family's literary tradition.

66.

The home's interiors include lavish wallpapers, rich textiles, and intricate details that capture the Victorian era's opulence.

67.

The house has been meticulously restored to its appearance during Twain's residency.

68.

The Mark Twain House & Museum was declared a National Historic Landmark in 1962.

69.

The property also includes the Mark Twain Museum Center, which features exhibits related to Twain's life, work, and legacy.

70.

The museum showcases artifacts, photographs, manuscripts, and personal belongings of Mark Twain and his family.

71.

The museum offers guided tours that provide insights into Mark Twain's life, his literary contributions, and the historical context of the era.

72.

The house's furnishings and decor reflect the tastes and preferences of Mark Twain's wife, Olivia Langdon Clemens.

73.

The Mark Twain House often hosts special events, lectures, and programs that celebrate literature and culture.

74.

The home's location in the Nook Farm neighborhood of Hartford placed Twain in the company of other prominent authors and intellectuals of the time.

75.

Twain's fondness for travel is evident in the house's decor, which includes items collected from his journeys around the world.

76.

The house's carriage house and stable complex were designed by Twain's friend, architect George Keller.

77.

The Clemens family entertained many notable guests and luminaries in the arts and politics at the Mark Twain House.

78.

Twain's connection to the house was profound, and he often referred to it as his "dream home."

79.

The family's love for animals is evident in the presence of a family of cats that resided on the property.

80.

The house showcases Twain's humor and wit through various quotes and inscriptions displayed throughout the interiors.

81.

In 1891, due to financial difficulties, the Clemens family was forced to move to Europe, and the house was sold.

82.

The house underwent various ownership changes and uses, including being turned into a boarding school for girls.

83.

In 1929, the house was purchased by The Mark Twain Memorial, a nonprofit organization dedicated to preserving the home and honoring Twain's legacy.

84.

The organization worked tirelessly to restore the house to its former glory and opened it to the public in 1974.

85.

The Mark Twain House is often considered one of the best-preserved historic homes of a major American author.

86.

The house's exterior features intricate wood carvings and decorative details that reflect the ornate Gothic Revival style.

87.

The house's conservatory, located off the library, was a favorite spot for Twain to read and relax.

88.

Twain's financial difficulties, stemming from investments and business ventures, impacted his ability to retain ownership of the house.

89.

The house's location in Hartford was strategic, as Twain was close to major publishing centers and cultural hubs.

90.

The Mark Twain House is a testament to the enduring legacy of Mark Twain and his contributions to American literature.

91.

The museum offers educational programs for students and teachers, encouraging an understanding of Twain's work in historical context.

92.

The house's decorative elements include intricate woodwork, plaster details, and elaborate ceiling designs.

93.

The Mark Twain House has served as an inspiration for writers, scholars, and visitors seeking to connect with Twain's genius.

94.

The museum offers special exhibitions that explore various aspects of Mark Twain's life and writings.

95.

The museum's gift shop features a variety of books, souvenirs, and items related to Mark Twain and his works.

96.

In recent years, efforts have been made to highlight the contributions of African American servants who worked in the house.

97.

The Mark Twain House is considered a must-visit destination for literary enthusiasts and those interested in American history.

98.

The museum's archival collections include letters, manuscripts, photographs, and documents related to Mark Twain's life and career.

99.

The Mark Twain House & Museum continues to contribute to literary scholarship and cultural awareness through its programs and exhibits.

100.

The preservation of the Mark Twain House ensures that the legacy of one of America's greatest authors will be cherished for generations to come.

101.

House centipedes (Scutigera coleoptrata) are arthropods belonging to the class Chilopoda and are not insects but rather part of the same group as centipedes.

102.

They are known for their distinctive appearance, featuring long, segmented bodies and numerous legs.

103.

Despite their name, house centipedes are found not only in houses but also in damp and dark environments like basements, bathrooms, and crawl spaces.

104.

House centipedes have a flattened body shape, which allows them to easily navigate through tight spaces.

105.

They typically have 15 pairs of long, delicate legs, giving them a total of 30 legs, although they can have as few as 15 pairs or as many as 177 pairs.

106.

The last pair of legs on a house centipede is much longer than the others, which helps them capture prey.

107.

House centipedes have a yellowish-gray to brown coloration with three dark stripes running down their back.

108.

Their antennae are long and slender, and their eyes are relatively simple.

109.

House centipedes are predators, primarily feeding on other insects, spiders, and small arthropods.

110.

They use their venomous fangs to inject paralyzing venom into their prey.

111.

Despite their venomous bite, house centipedes are not dangerous to humans. Their venom is not harmful to people and is primarily used to immobilize prey.

112.

House centipedes are known for their speed and agility, which helps them catch fast-moving insects.

113.

They prefer damp environments and are often found in basements, bathrooms, kitchens, and other areas with high humidity.

114.

House centipedes are nocturnal creatures, usually coming out at night to hunt for food.

115.

They are considered beneficial to have in homes as they help control populations of other pests like spiders and cockroaches.

116.

House centipedes are not social insects and are generally solitary creatures.

117.

They communicate primarily through vibrations and chemical signals.

118.

House centipedes reproduce by laying eggs in small, hidden crevices. The female may guard her eggs until they hatch.

119.

After hatching, the young house centipedes resemble miniature versions of the adults and go through several molting stages before reaching maturity.

120.

House centipedes can live up to three years.

121.

They are found in various parts of the world, including North America, Europe, and Asia.

122.

House centipedes have a unique way of moving called "alternating tripod" movement, where they use three pairs of legs at a time to create a steady motion.

123.

They are sensitive to light and will often seek out dark and hidden areas during the day.

124.

House centipedes have a strong aversion to dry environments, which is why they are commonly found in damp places.

125.

They are not destructive pests and do not damage structures or belongings.

126.

House centipedes are not considered aggressive toward humans, and they will typically flee if encountered.

127.

If threatened, a house centipede may use its speed and agility to escape to a hiding place.

128.

House centipedes have been around for millions of years, with fossils dating back to the Devonian period.

129.

Despite their somewhat alarming appearance, house centipedes are harmless to pets and are not known to cause any significant harm.

130.

They are voracious predators and can capture prey much larger than themselves, using their speed and venomous bite.

131.

House centipedes undergo a process called molting, where they shed their exoskeleton to allow for growth.

132.

The presence of house centipedes could indicate an underlying pest problem, as they are attracted to areas with abundant prey.

133.

Their presence can also be an indicator of moisture issues in a home, as they prefer humid environments.

134.

House centipedes have been known to occasionally bite humans, but the bites are generally minor and cause only mild pain or irritation.

135.

They are excellent climbers and can easily move up walls, across ceilings, and through tight spaces.

136.

House centipedes have an excellent sense of touch and use their long antennae to detect vibrations in their environment.

137.

In some cultures, house centipedes are considered symbols of luck or good fortune.

138.

House centipedes are not attracted to human food sources and do not consume pantry items.

139.

Their primary diet consists of insects, spiders, and other small arthropods.

140.

House centipedes have adapted to urban environments and can be found in both residential and commercial spaces.

141.

They are more commonly encountered in older homes with damp basements and crawl spaces.

142.

House centipedes are typically not seen in large numbers within a single area, as their population density is relatively low.

143.

Contrary to some myths, house centipedes do not crawl into people's ears or lay eggs inside homes.

144.

Their presence in a home can be managed by addressing moisture issues, sealing entry points, and reducing other pest populations.

145.

House centipedes are not social insects and do not engage in any form of group behavior or cooperation.

146.

In certain cultures, house centipedes are considered useful spirits that protect homes from negative energies.

147.

Despite their appearance, house centipedes are fragile creatures and can be easily injured or killed.

148.

House centipedes are not known to transmit diseases to humans.

149.

The number of legs on a house centipede can vary greatly, even within the same species.

150.

While house centipedes may startle homeowners with their sudden appearance, they play an important role in maintaining ecosystem balance by controlling insect populations.

151.

Howler monkeys are large New World monkeys belonging to the family Atelidae and the subfamily Alouattinae.

152.

They are known for their distinctive vocalizations, which can be heard over long distances and are among the loudest sounds produced by any animal.

153.

Howler monkeys are found in Central and South America, inhabiting rainforests, deciduous forests, and mangrove swamps.

154.

There are nine recognized species of howler monkeys, each with its own unique characteristics and distribution range.

155.

The mantled howler monkey (Alouatta palliata) is one of the most common and widely distributed species.

156.

Howler monkeys have a prehensile tail, which means their tail is adapted for grasping and can be used to hold onto branches while they move through the trees.

157.

Their tails are also used as a fifth limb for support and balance while they navigate through the trees.

158.

Howler monkeys have a stocky body with a robust build, and they can weigh up to 22 pounds (10 kilograms) or more.

159.

Their fur can range from reddish-brown to black, depending on the species.

160.

Howler monkeys are folivores, meaning their primary diet consists of leaves, but they also consume fruits, flowers, and occasionally insects.

161.

Their digestive system is specially adapted to break down tough plant materials like leaves.

162.

Howler monkeys have a multi-chambered stomach that aids in fermentation and digestion of their high-fiber diet.

163.

Howler monkeys have a unique feature called the hyoid bone, which is enlarged and helps amplify their vocalizations.

164.

Their vocalizations are used for communication within the troop, maintaining territory boundaries, and attracting potential mates.

165.

Male howler monkeys are the primary vocalizers and use their powerful calls to announce their presence and deter rival males.

166.

Howler monkeys' calls can be heard up to three miles (5 kilometers) away in the dense rainforest.

167.

Each howler monkey troop has its own distinct vocal signature, allowing individuals to identify members of their own group.

168.

Howler monkeys are known for their strong social bonds and typically live in multi-male, multi-female groups.

169.

Group sizes can vary from a few individuals to over 20, depending on factors like food availability and territory size.

170.

Howler monkeys have a complex social structure with dominant males and a hierarchy among both males and females.

171.

Their groups are matrilineal, meaning females remain in the group they were born into, while males typically disperse to other groups.

172.

Howler monkeys spend most of their lives in the trees and are skilled climbers, using their prehensile tail and strong limbs to move through the forest canopy.

173.

They have excellent depth perception, allowing them to accurately judge distances while leaping between branches.

174.

Howler monkeys are known for their slow and deliberate movements, rarely needing to move quickly due to their specialized diet and arboreal lifestyle.

175.

Their front limbs are longer than their hind limbs, which is an adaptation for swinging through the trees (brachiation).

176.

Howler monkeys have a gestation period of around six months, and females usually give birth to a single offspring.

177.

Infant howler monkeys cling to their mother's belly for the first few months of life, gradually transitioning to riding on her back.

178.

The mother provides care and protection for her young, grooming them and ensuring their safety within the group.

179.

Howler monkeys have a relatively slow reproductive rate, with females typically giving birth once every two to three years.

180.

Howler monkeys play a crucial role in forest ecosystems by dispersing seeds from the fruits they consume, contributing to the growth of new plants.

181.

They have a lifespan of around 20 to 30 years in the wild.

182.

Howler monkeys have few natural predators due to their large size and vocal abilities. Jaguars and large birds of prey are among their potential threats.

183.

Despite their intimidating appearance, howler monkeys are generally not aggressive toward humans and prefer to avoid contact.

184.

Habitat loss and fragmentation, as well as hunting for their meat and capture for the pet trade, pose significant threats to howler monkey populations.

185.

Some howler monkey species are listed as vulnerable or endangered on the International Union for Conservation of Nature (IUCN) Red List of Threatened Species.

186.

Conservation efforts focus on protecting their natural habitats and raising awareness about their ecological importance.

187.

Howler monkeys have a keen sense of smell, which they use to locate ripe fruits and potential food sources.

188.

Howler monkeys have a small, non-prehensile thumb, which differentiates them from other primates like spider monkeys.

189.

Their thumb is used for grasping objects and branches, while their other digits are adapted for gripping.

190.

Howler monkeys' molars are broad and flat, designed for crushing and grinding tough plant materials.

191.

In some cultures, howler monkeys are considered sacred animals and are protected from hunting and harm.

192.

Howler monkeys are active during the day (diurnal) and spend much of their time resting, grooming, and foraging for food.

193.

Their long fur helps protect them from rain and insects, while their dense undercoat provides insulation.

194.

Howler monkeys are essential components of the ecosystems they inhabit, contributing to nutrient cycling and plant diversity.

195.

In scientific research, howler monkeys have been studied for their vocalizations and social behaviors, providing insights into primate communication and group dynamics.

196.

Howler monkeys have well-developed color vision, helping them distinguish between ripe and unripe fruits.

197.

The first digit on their feet is opposable, allowing them to grasp branches securely while moving.

198.

Howler monkeys are considered a flagship species for rainforest conservation due to their iconic status and role in maintaining forest health.

199.

They are also considered bioindicators, reflecting the overall health of their habitat based on their population size and behavior.

200.

Observing howler monkeys in their natural habitat can provide valuable insights into the complex interactions of rainforest ecosystems and the importance of protecting them.

201.

Edward Jones was founded in 1922 by Edward D. Jones Sr. in St. Louis, Missouri, USA.

202.

The company's original focus was on providing investment services to individual investors in rural communities.

203.

Edward Jones' mission has always been to provide personalized, face-to-face financial advice and services.

204.

The company's first office was located in the basement of the Exchange National Bank building in St. Louis.

205.

Edward Jones' early clientele included teachers, farmers, and workers who often didn't have access to urban financial services.

206.

The firm's business model emphasized a strong commitment to building long-term relationships with clients.

207.

Edward D. Jones Sr. believed in putting clients' interests first and providing transparent investment advice.

208.

The company's famous slogan, "Making Sense of Investing," reflects its dedication to simplifying complex financial matters for clients.

209.

In the early days, Edward Jones focused on selling stocks, bonds, and mutual funds to individual investors.

210.

Edward D. Jones Sr. passed away in 1948, but the firm continued to grow under the leadership of Ted Jones, his son.

211.

Ted Jones expanded the company's reach beyond rural communities, opening offices in more suburban and urban areas.

212.

In 1971, the firm transitioned to a partnership structure to ensure alignment between financial advisors and the firm's goals.

213.

In 1979, John Bachmann became the managing partner of Edward Jones and played a significant role in its growth and development.

214.

Edward Jones is known for its unique business model, where financial advisors are referred to as "financial advisors," not brokers.

215.

The company's financial advisors often establish one-on-one relationships with clients, which contributes to their high level of trust.

216.

Edward Jones has a decentralized structure, with each branch office run by a financial advisor responsible for managing relationships in their local community.

217.

In 1980, the company established the Edward Jones Trust Company to provide trust and estate services to clients.

218.

Throughout the 1980s and 1990s, Edward Jones continued to expand its services and branch network across the United States.

219.

In 1993, Edward Jones launched the Bridge Builder mutual funds, offering clients access to diversified investment options.

220.

The company's growth was marked by consistent focus on conservative investment strategies and disciplined financial planning.

221.

In 1995, Edward Jones expanded its business internationally by opening its first office in Canada.

222.

The company's client-centric approach earned it a reputation for excellent customer service and personalized financial advice.

223.

In 2000, Edward Jones established the Edward Jones Trust Company to provide trust and estate services to clients.

224.

Edward Jones was one of the first financial services firms to create a formal program to help clients plan for retirement.

225.

Despite the dot-com bubble and other economic challenges, Edward Jones maintained its focus on long-term investing strategies.

226.

In 2007, the company launched its Edward Jones Money Market Fund, providing clients with a safe and liquid investment option.

227.

Edward Jones' headquarters in St. Louis is known for its unique architecture and campus-like setting.

228.

During the 2008 financial crisis, Edward Jones remained committed to its principles of conservative investing and client-centered advice.

229.

The company continued to grow throughout the recession, opening new offices and expanding its client base.

230.

In 2012, Penny Pennington became the firm's first female managing partner, reinforcing the company's commitment to diversity and inclusion.

231.

Edward Jones places a strong emphasis on corporate social responsibility, supporting various community and charitable initiatives.

232.

The firm provides ongoing training and professional development for its financial advisors, ensuring they have the skills and knowledge needed to serve clients effectively.

233.

Edward Jones has consistently ranked high on lists of best places to work, emphasizing its supportive and inclusive company culture.

234.

The company has received recognition for its efforts in promoting workplace diversity and equality.

235.

Edward Jones is known for its annual "Summer Regional Meetings," where financial advisors gather to discuss strategies, network, and learn from industry experts.

236.

In recent years, Edward Jones has expanded its digital offerings to provide clients with online tools and resources while maintaining its commitment to personalized advice.

237.

The firm continues to adapt to changing technology while retaining its core values and principles.

238.

As of 2021, Edward Jones has more than 12,000 branch offices serving clients in the United States and Canada.

239.

The company's financial advisors are supported by a team of experts in areas such as investment research, compliance, and technology.

240.

Edward Jones is a leader in providing retirement planning and investment services to individual investors, helping them achieve their financial goals.

241.

The firm offers a range of investment options, including stocks, bonds, mutual funds, exchange-traded funds (ETFs), and annuities.

242.

Edward Jones has a strong commitment to financial literacy and education, offering resources and workshops to help clients make informed decisions.

243.

The company's research team provides regular market insights and analysis to help clients understand current market trends.

244.

Edward Jones has received numerous awards and accolades for its excellence in customer service and its commitment to ethical practices.

245.

The company emphasizes a values-based approach to investing, helping clients align their investments with their personal values and beliefs.

246.

Edward Jones has a long-standing tradition of community involvement, with financial advisors often engaged in local charitable initiatives.

247.

The firm's investment philosophy is based on a disciplined, long-term approach, aiming to provide consistent returns over time.

248.

Edward Jones is a strong advocate for retirement planning, helping clients navigate the complexities of saving and investing for their future.

249.

The company's commitment to personalized service has contributed to its reputation as a trusted partner in clients' financial journeys.

250.

Edward Jones remains dedicated to its founding principles of putting clients first, providing personalized advice, and helping individuals achieve their financial goals.

251.

Sherwin-Williams was founded in 1866 by Henry Sherwin and Edward Williams in Cleveland, Ohio, USA.

252.

The company initially began as a partnership between Sherwin, a trained chemist, and Williams, a businessman.

253.

Sherwin-Williams' early products included ready-mixed paints and varnishes, which were revolutionary at the time.

254.

In 1870, Sherwin-Williams introduced the first ready-mixed paint in cans, making it easier for consumers to buy and use.

255.

The company's logo, the "Cover the Earth" globe, was introduced in 1894 and symbolizes Sherwin-Williams' global presence.

256.

Sherwin-Williams played a significant role in developing and promoting the use of paint in the emerging automobile industry.

257.

The company's research and development efforts led to the development of many innovative paint products and technologies.

258.

In the early 20th century, Sherwin-Williams introduced the first paint color cards, helping customers choose colors for their homes.

259.

Sherwin-Williams' paint was used on the famous "Spirit of St. Louis" airplane flown by Charles Lindbergh in his historic transatlantic flight.

260.

During World War II, the company produced camouflage paints for military vehicles and equipment.

261.

Sherwin-Williams expanded internationally in the 1950s, opening stores in Canada and other countries.

262.

The company has a strong commitment to sustainability, including efforts to reduce its environmental impact and promote eco-friendly products.

263.

In 1968, Sherwin-Williams introduced SuperPaint, a product that combined paint and primer in one, saving time and effort for consumers.

264.

The company's acquisitions have played a significant role in its growth, including the purchase of Dutch Boy Paints in 1980.

265.

In the 1990s, Sherwin-Williams introduced the Harmony line of paints, which was one of the first eco-friendly paints with low VOC (volatile organic compounds) content.

266.

Sherwin-Williams has a long history of supporting communities through charitable initiatives and partnerships.

267.

The company's involvement in the automotive industry led to the creation of automotive finishes that are still widely used today.

268.

Sherwin-Williams' paint products have been used in numerous iconic landmarks and buildings around the world.

269.

The company introduced the HGTV Home by Sherwin-Williams paint line, offering consumers a curated selection of on-trend colors.

270.

In 2017, Sherwin-Williams acquired Valspar Corporation, expanding its product offerings and global reach.

271.

Sherwin-Williams has a dedicated team of color experts who predict and set color trends for each year.

272.

The company's ColorSnap Visualizer app allows users to virtually "try on" different paint colors in their own spaces before making a decision.

273.

Sherwin-Williams' Pro Painters Program provides professional painters with tools, resources, and discounts to help them succeed.

274.

The company's product portfolio includes paints, stains, coatings, and a wide range of application tools and accessories.

275.

Sherwin-Williams' commitment to quality and innovation has earned it recognition as an industry leader.

276.

The company's headquarters in Cleveland, Ohio, is located in a LEED-certified building that reflects its sustainability values.

277.

Sherwin-Williams has a strong presence on social media platforms, engaging with consumers and sharing design inspiration.

278.

The company is known for its dedication to customer service, providing expert advice and solutions to help customers achieve their vision.

279.

Sherwin-Williams' involvement in community initiatives includes projects that revitalize neighborhoods through paint and beautification efforts.

280.

The company's diverse product offerings cater to both residential and commercial customers, making it a trusted choice in various industries.

281.

Sherwin-Williams has been recognized for its efforts in diversity and inclusion, fostering a culture of equality within the organization.

282.

The company's research and development centers work on creating innovative products that meet the evolving needs of customers.

283.

Sherwin-Williams has a long-standing commitment to producing paints and coatings that are safe for both consumers and the environment.

284.

The company's dedication to quality has led to partnerships with major retailers and contractors worldwide.

285.

Sherwin-Williams provides color consulting services to help customers choose the perfect shades for their spaces.

286.

The company's online resources include paint calculators, how-to videos, and DIY project ideas.

287.

Sherwin-Williams' stores often feature interactive displays and color selection tools to enhance the shopping experience.

288.

The company's emphasis on employee development and training has contributed to its success as an industry leader.

289.

Sherwin-Williams' iconic "Cover the Earth" globe logo is recognized globally and symbolizes the company's expansive reach.

290.

The company is known for its commitment to manufacturing high-quality paints and coatings in its own facilities.

291.

Sherwin-Williams is actively involved in promoting sustainable building practices through its product offerings.

292.

The company's Color of the Year selections influence design trends in various industries, including interior design and fashion.

293.

Sherwin-Williams is involved in philanthropic efforts that support education, health, and community development.

294.

The company's website offers a vast library of paint colors and tools to inspire and assist customers in their projects.

295.

Sherwin-Williams has a robust online community where customers can share their projects, ask questions, and seek advice.

296.

The company's innovation extends beyond paints, as it also develops advanced coating solutions for industrial applications.

297.

Sherwin-Williams' commitment to environmental responsibility includes efforts to reduce waste and promote recycling.

298.

The company's reputation for quality has led to long-standing partnerships with contractors and professionals.

299.

Sherwin-Williams' dedication to excellence and customer satisfaction has earned it numerous awards and recognition.

300.

Throughout its history, Sherwin-Williams has remained committed to its founding principles of quality, innovation, and customer service.

301.

The Joseph Webb House, also known as the Silas Deane House, was built in 1752 for Joseph Webb, a prominent merchant, politician, and Patriot during the American Revolution.

302.

The house is a prime example of Georgian architecture, characterized by its symmetrical design, formal proportions, and decorative elements.

303.

Joseph Webb was a close friend of Silas Deane, a diplomat and a delegate to the Continental Congress, which is why the house is also referred to as the Silas Deane House.

304.

The Joseph Webb House is a National Historic Landmark and is listed on the National Register of Historic Places.

305.

The house played a significant role in the American Revolutionary War, serving as a meeting place for Patriot leaders and a site for secret negotiations.

306.

Joseph Webb's wife, Mehitabel, was known for her hospitality, and the house hosted many important figures of the time, including George Washington and Benjamin Franklin.

307.

The house's interior features authentic period furnishings, providing visitors with a glimpse into colonial life and the Revolutionary era.

308.

The Joseph Webb House is managed and preserved by the Webb-Deane-Stevens Museum, which also includes the Silas Deane House and the Isaac Stevens House.

309.

The museum offers guided tours that provide historical context and stories about the people who lived in the Joseph Webb House.

310.

The house's formal garden reflects the gardening practices of the 18th century and is a lovely example of a colonial-era landscape.

311.

The Joseph Webb House has been carefully restored to its 18th-century appearance, with original woodwork, paneling, and architectural details.

312.

The house's ballroom was the setting for many social events and gatherings during the colonial period.

313.

Joseph Webb was involved in the shipping and mercantile business, contributing to the economic development of Wethersfield.

314.

The Webb-Deane-Stevens Museum offers educational programs and events that bring history to life for visitors of all ages.

315.

The house's historical significance extends beyond the American Revolution, as it provides insights into colonial architecture, craftsmanship, and daily life.

316.

The Joseph Webb House has been featured in documentaries, books, and articles that highlight its role in American history.

317.

The house's architecture showcases elements such as a steeply pitched roof, dormer windows, and decorative pilasters.

318.

A unique feature of the Joseph Webb House is its hipped roof, a departure from the more common gable roofs of the time.

319.

The house's interiors include period furnishings, artwork, and artifacts that illustrate the tastes and lifestyles of its inhabitants.

320.

Joseph Webb was active in local government and served as a selectman, contributing to the community's growth and development.

321.

The Webb-Deane-Stevens Museum offers special events and reenactments that transport visitors back in time to the colonial era.

322.

The Joseph Webb House's location in Wethersfield, one of Connecticut's oldest towns, adds to its historical significance.

323.

The house's cellar provides a glimpse into daily life in colonial times, with displays of period tools, implements, and storage areas.

324.

The Joseph Webb House's historical authenticity and educational programs make it a popular destination for school groups and educational tours.

325.

The museum offers workshops and demonstrations on various colonial-era activities, including hearth cooking and textile arts.

326.

The Joseph Webb House's preservation efforts include ongoing research, conservation work, and maintenance of its historical accuracy.

327.

The house's rooms are furnished with items that belonged to the Webb family, creating a sense of connection to the past.

328.

The Webb-Deane-Stevens Museum's collection includes artifacts related to the American Revolution, giving visitors a deeper understanding of the era.

329.

The Joseph Webb House's role as a center of social and political activity during the Revolutionary period underscores its importance in American history.

330.

The museum's gift shop offers a selection of books, souvenirs, and items related to colonial life and history.

331.

The Joseph Webb House's architecture and historical significance have made it a source of inspiration for preservationists and historians.

332.

The house's location along the historic Washington-Rochambeau Revolutionary Route (W3R) adds to its connections to American history.

333.

The Joseph Webb House's gardens are designed to reflect colonial-era horticulture practices and include plants commonly grown during that time.

334.

The museum's educational outreach includes partnerships with schools, libraries, and community organizations to promote historical awareness.

335.

The Joseph Webb House has been the setting for academic research and historical studies that contribute to the understanding of colonial life.

336.

The museum's commitment to preserving and sharing history extends to collaborating with other cultural institutions and historical sites.

337.

The Joseph Webb House's association with influential figures of the American Revolution underscores its role in shaping the nation's history.

338.

The house's architectural details, such as its pedimented doorways and intricate woodwork, highlight the craftsmanship of the time.

339.

The museum's dedication to historical accuracy and authenticity allows visitors to immerse themselves in the past.

340.

The Joseph Webb House's connection to important events of the Revolutionary period contributes to its recognition as a valuable historical site.

341.

The house's interpretation of history includes exploring the perspectives of various individuals who lived during the colonial era.

342.

The museum's guided tours provide insights into the stories of the Webb family, their guests, and the historical events they witnessed.

343.

The Joseph Webb House's collections include period textiles, ceramics, and decorative arts that offer insights into daily life.

344.

The museum's emphasis on public engagement and interactive experiences helps visitors connect with history on a personal level.

345.

The Joseph Webb House's inclusion in the National Historic Landmark program acknowledges its exceptional historical and cultural significance.

346.

The house's location in the heart of Wethersfield's historic district allows visitors to explore other nearby historic sites and attractions.

347.

The museum's commitment to research and scholarship ensures that the history presented is based on accurate and well-documented information.

348.

The Joseph Webb House's educational programs encompass a wide range of topics, from colonial clothing to Revolutionary War espionage.

349.

The museum's events, workshops, and lectures encourage ongoing dialogue and exploration of America's colonial past.

350.

The Joseph Webb House's historical value lies not only in its physical structure but also in the stories it preserves and shares about the people and events that shaped early American history.

351.

The Noah Webster Birthplace is the birthplace and childhood home of Noah Webster, born on October 16, 1758.

352.

Noah Webster is best known for his work on the American Dictionary of the English Language, which significantly influenced American English.

353.

The house is a colonial-style farmhouse built in 1736 and is an excellent example of early Connecticut architecture.

354.

The birthplace is a National Historic Landmark and is listed on the National Register of Historic Places.

355.

The house was constructed by Noah Webster's father, Noah Sr., who was a farmer and local civic leader.

356.

The Noah Webster Birthplace Association was formed in 1971 to preserve and interpret the historic site.

357.

The birthplace serves as a museum dedicated to preserving the legacy of Noah Webster and his contributions to American language and culture.

358.

The house features period furnishings, including furniture and household items from the 18th century.

359.

Visitors to the birthplace can explore the rooms where Noah Webster spent his early years and learn about his upbringing.

360.

The birthplace's guided tours offer insights into the Webster family's daily life and the historical context of the time.

361.

Noah Webster was a strong advocate for American nationalism and believed that a distinct American identity could be fostered through language.

362.

In addition to his dictionary work, Noah Webster authored grammar books, spelling books, and textbooks that were widely used in early American education.

363.

The museum's exhibits highlight Noah Webster's impact on American education, language, and culture.

364.

The birthplace's location in West Hartford is also the site of the Noah Webster House and West Hartford Historical Society.

365.

The house's architectural details include a central chimney, steep pitched roof, and clapboard siding.

366.

The birthplace's educational programs engage visitors of all ages with interactive activities, workshops, and special events.

367.

Noah Webster's efforts to standardize American spelling and pronunciation are reflected in his dictionary entries and linguistic principles.

368.

The museum's collection includes artifacts related to Noah Webster's life and work, including original editions of his publications.

369.

The birthplace offers virtual and on-site educational experiences, making its resources accessible to a wider audience.

370.

The Noah Webster Birthplace Association is committed to ongoing research and scholarship related to Noah Webster's legacy.

371.

The house's location in New England allows visitors to experience the region's colonial history and heritage.

372.

Noah Webster's dictionary contained over 70,000 words and definitions, many of which were of American origin.

373.

The birthplace's exhibits delve into Noah Webster's role as a political commentator, educator, and language reformer.

374.

The museum's programs explore the evolution of the English language and its impact on American society.

375.

The Noah Webster Birthplace Association collaborates with educators to develop curriculum materials related to language, history, and culture.

376.

The birthplace's gardens and grounds reflect the agricultural practices of the 18th century.

377.

The museum's gift shop offers a selection of books, gifts, and educational materials related to language and history.

378.

The Noah Webster Birthplace Association organizes events that celebrate language, culture, and the legacy of Noah Webster.

379.

The birthplace serves as a resource for scholars, researchers, and educators interested in American language history.

380.

Noah Webster's efforts to simplify and standardize spelling in American English aimed to make reading and writing more accessible to all.

381.

The birthplace's educational initiatives extend beyond its physical location through online resources and outreach programs.

382.

The museum's exhibits explore the impact of Noah Webster's dictionary on American literature, education, and communication.

383.

The Noah Webster Birthplace is a place of historical significance and reflection on the evolution of language and communication.

384.

The house's proximity to Hartford, Connecticut's capital, provides visitors with opportunities to explore the city's cultural attractions.

385.

Noah Webster's dictionary was one of the earliest comprehensive dictionaries of the English language in the United States.

386.

The museum's commitment to fostering an appreciation for language and history aligns with Noah Webster's own educational philosophy.

387.

The Noah Webster Birthplace Association relies on community support and partnerships to continue its preservation and educational efforts.

388.

The house's location within a historic New England town allows visitors to experience a sense of continuity with the past.

389.

Noah Webster's work on language reform aimed to create a distinct American identity through linguistic independence from British English.

390.

The birthplace's exhibits explore the history of language dictionaries and their role in documenting cultural changes.

391.

The museum's interpretation of Noah Webster's life and work emphasizes his influence on American language and educational practices.

392.

The Noah Webster Birthplace's connection to the history of American publishing underscores its significance in American cultural history.

393.

Noah Webster's dictionary included definitions and explanations of American political and legal terms.

394.

The museum's outreach programs extend to schools, libraries, and educational institutions to promote language awareness and history.

395.

The birthplace's location in New England offers visitors opportunities to explore other historic sites and attractions in the region.

396.

Noah Webster's advocacy for spelling reform included proposals to simplify spelling and eliminate silent letters in words.

397.

The museum's commitment to preserving the birthplace and promoting linguistic education aligns with contemporary discussions about language and communication.

398.

The Noah Webster Birthplace Association engages volunteers and supporters in its efforts to maintain and enhance the site.

399.

The birthplace's programs encourage visitors to think critically about language and its role in shaping culture and society.

400.

The Noah Webster Birthplace serves as a testament to the enduring legacy of Noah Webster and his contributions to American language, education, and identity.

401.

The Humboldt Penguin (Spheniscus humboldti) is a medium-sized species of penguin native to the coasts of South America, particularly along the Pacific Ocean.

402.

Named after the German explorer and scientist Alexander von Humboldt, these penguins are also known as Peruvian Penguins or Chilean Penguins.

403.

Humboldt Penguins are classified as a vulnerable species due to threats like habitat destruction, overfishing, and climate change.

404.

These penguins have a distinctive black band running across their chest, with white undersides and a black head and upper body.

405.

Humboldt Penguins have pink patches of skin around their eyes, which become brighter when they are excited or during mating displays.

406.

They have strong, flipper-like wings that are adapted for swimming rather than flying, which makes them excellent swimmers.

407.

Humboldt Penguins are expert divers and can reach depths of up to 150 meters (492 feet) while foraging for food.

408.

Their diet primarily consists of small fish, squid, and crustaceans, which they catch using their sharp beaks.

409.

Unlike some other penguin species, Humboldt Penguins mainly feed during the day and return to their nests at night.

410.

These penguins have a unique braying call that sounds similar to a donkey's bray, which they use for communication and to locate their mates.

411.

Humboldt Penguins are social birds and usually form colonies, often sharing nesting sites with other bird species like seagulls.

412.

They are known for their elaborate courtship rituals, which involve displays of affection and mutual preening.

413.

Humboldt Penguins typically nest in burrows or under bushes to protect their eggs and chicks from predators and extreme weather conditions.

414.

Both parents take turns incubating the eggs and caring for the chicks once they hatch.

415.

Chicks have a grayish downy covering that gradually changes to the adult coloration as they grow older.

416.

Humboldt Penguins have specialized salt glands above their eyes to help them excrete excess salt, which is essential for their survival in marine environments.

417.

These penguins can swim at speeds of around 20 miles per hour (32 kilometers per hour) when they're hunting for food.

418.

They have excellent vision both underwater and on land, allowing them to locate prey and predators efficiently.

419.

Humboldt Penguins have strong beaks with backward-facing spines that help them hold onto slippery prey.

420.

In the wild, their lifespan is usually around 15 to 20 years, while in captivity, they can live even longer.

421.

Humboldt Penguins are found along the Pacific coasts of South America, from central Chile to northern Peru.

422.

They prefer rocky shorelines and cliffs where they can build their nests and find shelter.

423.

The population of Humboldt Penguins has declined significantly due to overfishing, habitat destruction, and climate change, which affects their prey availability.

424.

Several conservation organizations and initiatives are working to protect and conserve Humboldt Penguins and their habitats.

425.

The main predators of Humboldt Penguins include larger birds of prey, such as gulls and skuas, as well as some marine mammals.

426.

Humboldt Penguins use their flippers to help regulate their body temperature, often holding them out to catch the sun or tucking them in to conserve heat.

427.

The penguins' waterproof feathers and layer of fat under their skin provide insulation and help them stay warm in cold water.

428.

Humboldt Penguins have unique patterns of spots and markings on their chests, which researchers use to identify and track individuals.

429.

These penguins have been observed forming lifelong bonds with their mates and returning to the same nesting sites year after year.

430.

Their habitat overlaps with various other marine species, contributing to the overall biodiversity of their coastal ecosystems.

431.

Humboldt Penguins have adapted to their environment by developing strong muscles for swimming and powerful flippers for steering underwater.

432.

One of the major threats to their survival is the depletion of their prey species due to overfishing.

433.

Humboldt Penguins are known for their comical waddle on land due to their upright posture and short legs.

434.

Conservation efforts often involve habitat restoration, education, and raising awareness about the importance of protecting these birds.

435.

Some Humboldt Penguins have been successfully bred and raised in captivity as part of conservation programs.

436.

These penguins often travel long distances to find food, and they may even migrate in search of better feeding grounds.

437.

In recent years, the establishment of marine protected areas has provided some degree of protection for Humboldt Penguins and their prey.

438.

They have well-developed hearing, which helps them communicate with other penguins and detect predators or threats.

439.

Humboldt Penguins have a streamlined body shape that reduces drag while swimming, allowing them to move efficiently through the water.

440.

Their diet can vary depending on the availability of prey in their environment, but fish like anchovies and sardines are common food sources.

441.

These penguins can spend several days at sea, covering long distances while foraging for food.

442.

The Humboldt Penguin is closely related to the Magellanic Penguin, and they share some similar characteristics and behaviors.

443.

Climate change is affecting the distribution of fish populations, potentially impacting the food sources of Humboldt Penguins.

444.

Human activities, such as pollution and oil spills, can have detrimental effects on the penguins' health and habitats.

445.

Humboldt Penguins are a popular attraction in zoos and aquariums, helping to raise awareness about their conservation status.

446.

In addition to their visual communication and calls, Humboldt Penguins use body movements to convey messages to each other.

447.

Their unique black and white coloration provides camouflage both in the water (from predators looking up) and on land (from predators looking down).

448.

The penguins' population decline has led to increased concern about their conservation status and the importance of protecting their habitats.

449.

The Humboldt Penguin is an iconic species that has become a symbol of the fragile coastal ecosystems of South America.

450.

The survival of Humboldt Penguins is not only essential for their own species but also for the overall health and balance of marine ecosystems along the Pacific coast of South America.

451.

Huntsman spiders belong to the family Sparassidae and are known for their large size, unique appearance, and hunting behavior.

452.

There are around 1,000 known species of huntsman spiders distributed across various regions of the world.

453.

These spiders are commonly called "huntsman" due to their hunting strategy of actively chasing and capturing their prey.

454.

Huntsman spiders have a flattened body shape with long legs that extend laterally, giving them a crab-like appearance.

455.

They are mostly found in warm and tropical regions, such as Australia, Africa, Asia, and the Americas.

456.

Despite their intimidating appearance, huntsman spiders are not considered dangerous to humans and are generally not aggressive.

457.

Huntsman spiders are known for their large leg span, which can reach up to 12 inches (30 centimeters) in some species.

458.

Unlike most spiders, huntsman spiders have excellent vision and can see well in dim light, which helps them hunt both day and night.

459.

Their eight eyes are arranged in two rows, with the front row having two large eyes for better depth perception.

460.

Huntsman spiders are known to take shelter in human homes and buildings, hiding in crevices and corners.

461.

They are skilled climbers and can walk on walls and ceilings, thanks to their specialized leg structure and adhesive foot pads.

462.

Despite their climbing ability, huntsman spiders don't create traditional webs to catch prey. Instead, they actively hunt for insects and other arthropods.

463.

When disturbed, huntsman spiders may run quickly to escape, often causing alarm due to their sudden movements.

464.

Huntsman spiders have a variety of colors and patterns, which can help them blend into their natural environment.

465.

Some huntsman spider species have adapted to urban environments and are commonly found indoors in homes and buildings.

466.

Huntsman spiders use their venom to immobilize their prey, which consists of insects like cockroaches, crickets, and moths.

467.

While their venom is not dangerous to humans, it can cause localized pain, swelling, and redness if bitten.

468.

Huntsman spiders are considered beneficial to ecosystems and gardens as they help control insect populations.

469.

The females of some huntsman species are known to carry their egg sacs with them, attached to their spinnerets or under their abdomen.

470.

Females guard their eggs until they hatch, and they may even provide some level of maternal care to the spiderlings.

471.

Spiderlings undergo several molts as they grow, shedding their exoskeleton to accommodate their increasing size.

472.

Huntsman spiders are ambush predators, relying on their speed and stealth to catch prey by surprise.

473.

Males and females often exhibit sexual dimorphism, with females generally larger and bulkier than males.

474.

Huntsman spiders possess specialized hairs on their legs called trichobothria, which help them detect vibrations and movements.

475.

In some cultures, huntsman spiders are considered symbols of good luck and are often spared when encountered indoors.

476.

Huntsman spiders are capable of regenerating lost limbs during molting cycles.

477.

These spiders can produce silk, but they use it primarily for creating shelters or draglines for personal use, rather than constructing webs.

478.

Despite their large size, huntsman spiders are relatively lightweight due to their thin exoskeleton.

479.

In some regions, huntsman spiders are considered valuable for pest control in agriculture.

480.

Huntsman spiders are often depicted in popular media, contributing to their reputation as both fearsome and fascinating creatures.

481.

The largest species of huntsman spiders are found in Australia and are known as the "giant huntsman spiders."

482.

Huntsman spiders have a unique method of capturing prey using their strong front legs to grasp and hold their victims.

483.

Some huntsman spider species are known to mimic bird droppings in order to avoid detection by predators.

484.

Unlike some other spider species, huntsman spiders don't build silk egg sacs but carry their eggs attached to their bodies.

485.

The lifespan of huntsman spiders varies depending on the species, but most live for about one to two years.

486.

The process of molting in huntsman spiders can take several hours and leaves them vulnerable to predation until their new exoskeleton hardens.

487.

Despite their name, not all huntsman spider species actively "hunt" their prey; some are more ambush-oriented.

488.

Huntsman spiders can produce silk through specialized spinnerets located at the end of their abdomen.

489.

Some huntsman spider species have been observed using vibrations to communicate with potential mates.

490.

The appearance of huntsman spiders can vary greatly between species, with some having striking patterns and colors.

491.

There have been documented cases of huntsman spiders catching and eating small vertebrates like geckos and small birds.

492.

Huntsman spiders are found in a wide range of habitats, including forests, grasslands, deserts, and urban areas.

493.

These spiders are often associated with warm climates, as they are ectothermic and require external sources of heat to be active.

494.

Huntsman spiders have been introduced to new regions through human activity, sometimes leading to ecological disruptions.

495.

The hairs on huntsman spiders' legs and bodies can be sensitive to touch and aid in detecting prey or predators.

496.

Some huntsman spiders have evolved to have flattened bodies that allow them to fit into tight spaces, enhancing their ability to hide.

497.

The size and appearance of huntsman spiders can lead to mistaken identity with potentially harmful spider species.

498.

Huntsman spiders have been the subject of scientific research due to their unique behaviors, adaptations, and roles in ecosystems.

499.

Certain huntsman spider species are valued in traditional medicine and cultural practices in different parts of the world.

500.

The diverse and fascinating characteristics of huntsman spiders continue to captivate the curiosity of scientists and arachnid enthusiasts alike.

501.

Qualcomm was founded on July 1, 1985, in San Diego, California, by Dr. Irwin Jacobs and six other co-founders.

502.

The company's name, "Qualcomm," stands for "QUALity COMMunications."

503.

Dr. Irwin Jacobs, a former professor of electrical engineering, played a pivotal role in the development of CDMA (Code Division Multiple Access) technology, which became a cornerstone of Qualcomm's success.

504.

Qualcomm's early focus was on developing wireless communication technologies and solutions for military and government applications.

505.

The company played a key role in the development and commercialization of CDMA technology, which allowed more users to share the same frequency spectrum.

506.

CDMA technology later became the foundation for many 3G and 4G cellular networks worldwide.

507.

Qualcomm introduced its first commercial CDMA-based mobile phone in 1995, paving the way for widespread adoption of the technology.

508.

Qualcomm's CDMA technology was considered revolutionary for its ability to provide better call quality and higher capacity in mobile networks.

509.

The company's innovations helped shape the transition from analog to digital cellular communication.

510.

In the early 2000s, Qualcomm introduced its BREW (Binary Runtime Environment for Wireless) platform, enabling developers to create and deploy applications for mobile devices.

511.

The acquisition of SnapTrack in 2000 allowed Qualcomm to enhance its position in the location-based services market.

512.

Qualcomm played a role in the development of the WCDMA (Wideband Code Division Multiple Access) standard, which is a key component of 3G mobile networks.

513.

Qualcomm's innovations in wireless technologies were crucial in the advancement of smartphones and mobile data services.

514.

The company's Snapdragon system-on-chip (SoC) processors revolutionized the mobile industry by integrating various components onto a single chip.

515.

Snapdragon processors powered many smartphones, providing high-performance computing and power efficiency.

516.

In 2010, Qualcomm introduced the Snapdragon 1 GHz chipset, marking a significant milestone in smartphone processing power.

517.

Qualcomm was one of the pioneers in 4G technology, with its Snapdragon processors supporting LTE (Long-Term Evolution) connectivity.

518.

The company's Snapdragon processors are used in a wide range of devices beyond smartphones, including tablets, laptops, and IoT (Internet of Things) devices.

519.

Qualcomm's contributions extended to Wi-Fi and Bluetooth technologies, enhancing wireless connectivity for various devices.

520.

The company has a strong focus on research and development, consistently investing in new technologies and innovations.

521.

Qualcomm's patent portfolio is extensive and covers a wide range of wireless communication technologies.

522.

The company has been involved in various legal disputes and patent battles with other tech giants over the use of its patented technologies.

523.

Qualcomm's inventions have significantly influenced the development of mobile communication standards and industry practices.

524.

The company has expanded its offerings beyond hardware, providing software solutions for automotive, healthcare, and other industries.

525.

Qualcomm's leadership in 5G technology has been instrumental in driving the deployment of faster and more advanced wireless networks.

526.

In 2018, Qualcomm introduced the Snapdragon X50 modem, one of the first commercial 5G modems.

527.

The company's contributions to 5G technology have set the stage for new possibilities in IoT, autonomous vehicles, and real-time communication.

528.

Qualcomm's collaborations with global technology companies and mobile operators have been essential in shaping the future of wireless communication.

529.

The acquisition of Atheros Communications in 2011 expanded Qualcomm's capabilities in Wi-Fi and networking technologies.

530.

Qualcomm's investments in research and development have resulted in numerous breakthroughs and advancements in wireless technologies.

531.

The company's Snapdragon processors are known for their integration of CPU, GPU, and AI capabilities on a single chip.

532.

Qualcomm has been at the forefront of advancements in mobile graphics processing, enhancing gaming and multimedia experiences.

533.

In addition to technological contributions, Qualcomm has been involved in philanthropic efforts and community initiatives.

534.

The company has participated in educational programs and initiatives to promote STEM (Science, Technology, Engineering, and Mathematics) education.

535.

Qualcomm's innovations have impacted industries beyond telecommunications, including healthcare, automotive, and smart cities.

536.

The company's contributions to wireless communication have facilitated global connectivity and transformed the way people communicate and access information.

537.

Qualcomm's commitment to standards-based technologies has been crucial in fostering interoperability and collaboration within the industry.

538.

The company's research centers and laboratories are spread across the United States and other countries, fostering innovation on a global scale.

539.

Qualcomm's Snapdragon processors have been instrumental in enabling advanced camera capabilities in smartphones, including image processing and AI-enhanced features.

540.

The company's wireless solutions have played a significant role in bringing internet connectivity to remote and underserved areas.

541.

Qualcomm has played an active role in advocating for responsible technology practices, including environmental sustainability and ethical considerations.

542.

The company's focus on energy efficiency and reduced power consumption has contributed to the sustainability of mobile devices.

543.

Qualcomm's advancements in wireless technology have led to increased productivity, accessibility, and economic growth worldwide.

544.

The company has received numerous awards and recognitions for its technological contributions, including patents and innovation awards.

545.

Qualcomm's collaborations with industry partners and standards organizations have led to the development of open and interoperable technologies.

546.

The company's expertise in wireless communication has positioned it as a thought leader in the field, contributing to industry discussions and conferences.

547.

Qualcomm's technologies have paved the way for the Internet of Things (IoT), enabling devices to communicate and share data seamlessly.

548.

The company's wireless solutions have been vital in emergency response situations, enabling communication during natural disasters and crises.

549.

Qualcomm's innovations have supported advancements in healthcare technology, including remote patient monitoring and telemedicine solutions.

550.

Throughout its history, Qualcomm's commitment to innovation, collaboration, and technological excellence has shaped the evolution of wireless communication and its impact on society.

551.

Kraft Heinz is a multinational food and beverage company formed through the merger of Kraft Foods and H.J. Heinz Company.

552.

The merger of Kraft Foods and H.J. Heinz was completed on July 2, 2015, creating one of the largest food and beverage companies in the world.

553.

Kraft Foods was founded in 1903 by James L. Kraft in Chicago, Illinois, as a cheese manufacturer.

554.

H.J. Heinz Company, founded in 1869 by Henry J. Heinz, began as a small food processing company producing horseradish and pickles.

555.

H.J. Heinz is famous for introducing the iconic "57 Varieties" slogan, despite having more than 57 products.

556.

The merger was orchestrated by 3G Capital and Berkshire Hathaway, resulting in the creation of The Kraft Heinz Company.

557.

Kraft Heinz has headquarters in Chicago, Illinois, and Pittsburgh, Pennsylvania.

558.

The company's portfolio includes a wide range of well-known food and beverage brands such as Kraft, Heinz, Oscar Mayer, Philadelphia, and more.

559.

The merger aimed to capitalize on the complementary nature of the product portfolios of Kraft Foods and H.J. Heinz.

560.

Kraft Heinz is known for its diverse product offerings, including condiments, snacks, dairy products, frozen foods, and beverages.

561.

The company operates globally, with products sold in more than 190 countries.

562.

Warren Buffett's Berkshire Hathaway and 3G Capital own significant stakes in Kraft Heinz.

563.

Kraft Heinz became a publicly traded company on the NASDAQ stock exchange under the ticker symbol "KHC."

564.

The company's iconic Heinz Ketchup is one of the best-selling condiments in the world.

565.

Kraft Macaroni & Cheese, often referred to as "Kraft Dinner" in Canada, has been a staple in many households for decades.

566.

Oscar Mayer, a subsidiary of Kraft Heinz, is well-known for its hot dogs, bacon, and lunch meat products.

567.

The merger was accompanied by efforts to streamline operations and reduce costs, leading to layoffs and facility closures.

568.

In 2019, Kraft Heinz announced a significant write-down of its assets, including brands like Kraft and Oscar Mayer.

569.

The company has faced challenges in adapting to changing consumer preferences for healthier and more natural food options.

570.

Kraft Heinz has taken steps to reformulate products to remove artificial colors and preservatives from some of its offerings.

571.

The company has introduced new product lines and acquisitions to diversify its portfolio, focusing on health and wellness trends.

572.

In 2020, Kraft Heinz unveiled its "Restoring Growth" plan, aiming to revitalize its brands and increase profitability.

573.

Kraft Heinz has also invested in digital and e-commerce initiatives to adapt to changing shopping habits.

574.

The company has a history of charitable initiatives, including food donation programs and community engagement.

575.

Kraft Heinz has faced criticism for certain marketing and product decisions, prompting efforts to address consumer concerns.

576.

Despite its challenges, Kraft Heinz remains a major player in the global food and beverage industry.

577.

The company has a strong presence in North America, but it also operates in markets around the world.

578.

Kraft Heinz has a commitment to sustainability, with initiatives to reduce its environmental impact and support responsible sourcing.

579.

The company's iconic brands and products have made it a recognizable name in households across generations.

580.

Kraft Heinz has participated in partnerships and collaborations with other companies and organizations to drive innovation.

581.

The company's advertising campaigns, featuring its well-known brands, have become part of popular culture.

582.

Kraft Heinz has faced competition from both traditional food companies and newer, more health-focused brands.

583.

The merger between Kraft Foods and H.J. Heinz was valued at approximately $46 billion.

584.

Kraft Heinz has a strong online and social media presence, engaging with consumers through various digital platforms.

585.

The company's management has undergone changes since the merger, with new leadership taking the helm.

586.

Kraft Heinz's product portfolio includes a variety of food options, from pantry staples to indulgent treats.

587.

The company's financial performance has experienced fluctuations due to changing market conditions and consumer preferences.

588.

Kraft Heinz's corporate social responsibility efforts include initiatives related to environmental sustainability, hunger relief, and community engagement.

589.

The company's iconic packaging and labeling have contributed to its brand recognition and market presence.

590.

Kraft Heinz has been involved in various philanthropic endeavors, supporting causes related to education, hunger relief, and disaster response.

591.

The merger between Kraft Foods and H.J. Heinz was one of the largest in the food industry at the time.

592.

Kraft Heinz operates a wide range of manufacturing facilities, distribution centers, and research and development centers.

593.

The company's commitment to quality and food safety is a key aspect of its operations.

594.

Kraft Heinz has explored partnerships and collaborations with startups and technology companies to drive innovation.

595.

The company has participated in advertising campaigns during major sports events, including the Super Bowl.

596.

Kraft Heinz's products are found in grocery stores, convenience stores, and restaurants worldwide.

597.

The company has been recognized for its efforts in sustainability and corporate responsibility by various industry organizations.

598.

Kraft Heinz's history reflects the evolution of the food industry and changing consumer preferences.

599.

The company's products have become an integral part of many cultural traditions and recipes.

600.

Kraft Heinz continues to adapt to changing market dynamics and consumer expectations to remain a relevant and influential player in the food and beverage industry.

601.

The Henry Whitfield House, also known as the Whitfield State Museum, is located in Guilford, Connecticut, USA.

602.

It is one of the oldest houses in Connecticut and is considered the oldest stone house in New England.

603.

The house was built in 1639 by Reverend Henry Whitfield, who was the leader of a group of English Puritans known as the "First Company."

604.

The house was constructed using local fieldstone and wooden beams, reflecting the architectural style of early Colonial homes.

605.

Henry Whitfield House served as both a residence and a gathering place for religious services during its early history.

606.

The house is a prime example of the "saltbox" architectural style, characterized by a steep pitched roof with a single-story rear extension.

607.

The saltbox design earned its name from its resemblance to a wooden box used to store salt.

608.

The Henry Whitfield House was designated as a National Historic Landmark in 1960.

609.

It is also known as the "Old Stone House" due to its unique construction material and design.

610.

The house has been preserved and restored to showcase its original 17th-century appearance and artifacts.

611.

The museum inside the house features exhibits related to the early history of Guilford, the Connecticut colony, and daily life in the 17th century.

612.

The Henry Whitfield House is managed by the State of Connecticut and is open to the public for tours.

613.

The house's interior showcases period furnishings and artifacts that provide insight into Colonial life.

614.

The grounds around the Henry Whitfield House include a Colonial herb garden and historic markers.

615.

The house's location offers panoramic views of the Guilford town green and Long Island Sound.

616.

The site is an important historical landmark, representing the settlement of early English colonists in Connecticut.

617.

The Henry Whitfield House is considered a well-preserved example of early American architecture and history.

618.

The house has been featured in literature and historical accounts of Connecticut's colonial past.

619.

Reverend Henry Whitfield, the founder of the house, was a prominent figure in the early establishment of Guilford.

620.

The house served as a fortified refuge during times of conflict, providing shelter to settlers during Native American attacks.

621.

The house's construction materials reflect the area's natural resources, including quarried stone and nearby timber.

622.

The Henry Whitfield House was used as a model for the design of other homes and buildings in the region.

623.

The museum offers educational programs and events for visitors of all ages, including demonstrations of Colonial skills and crafts.

624.

The site has been used for historical reenactments to bring the past to life for modern audiences.

625.

The Henry Whitfield House provides a glimpse into the challenges and daily life of early settlers in Connecticut.

626.

The house's historical significance extends beyond its architectural features to its role in the development of the Guilford community.

627.

The museum staff and volunteers work to ensure the preservation and interpretation of the house's history.

628.

The Henry Whitfield House offers a unique opportunity for visitors to step back in time and experience early American life.

629.

The house has been featured in documentaries and television programs exploring American history and architecture.

630.

The site is a popular destination for school field trips and educational programs focused on Colonial history.

631.

The Henry Whitfield House has played a part in archaeological research to better understand the lives of early settlers.

632.

The museum regularly hosts events that celebrate Guilford's history and its role in the founding of Connecticut.

633.

The house's significance goes beyond its architectural value; it represents the cultural and historical roots of the region.

634.

The Henry Whitfield House is a reminder of the challenges faced by the first colonists as they established communities in the New World.

635.

Visitors to the house can explore its rooms and exhibits to learn about the different aspects of Colonial life, from food to clothing.

636.

The saltbox architecture of the house showcases the practical and resourceful nature of early settlers.

637.

The museum offers a sense of connection to the past, helping visitors understand the historical context of their own lives.

638.

The Henry Whitfield House has been an inspiration for artists and historians studying early American architecture.

639.

The site's location near the coast highlights the maritime connections that shaped the region's history.

640.

The museum's educational programs include hands-on activities that engage visitors in learning about Colonial life.

641.

The Henry Whitfield House has undergone preservation efforts to maintain its structural integrity and historical accuracy.

642.

The house is surrounded by scenic landscapes and gardens that reflect the natural beauty of Connecticut.

643.

The site's preservation contributes to the cultural heritage and identity of the Guilford community.

644.

The Henry Whitfield House offers a tangible link to the stories and experiences of the people who lived there centuries ago.

645.

The museum's exhibits include artifacts such as tools, household items, and documents that provide insights into everyday life.

646.

The house is a testament to the determination and resilience of early settlers as they established a new way of life.

647.

The Henry Whitfield House has been referenced in literature, historical accounts, and educational materials about Connecticut's past.

648.

The site's historical interpretation offers visitors a chance to engage with history in a tangible and immersive way.

649.

The museum's staff and volunteers are dedicated to preserving and sharing the history of the Henry Whitfield House with the public.

650.

The Henry Whitfield House stands as a living monument to the past, inviting visitors to explore the history and heritage of early colonial America.

651.

The Austin F. Williams Carriagehouse and House is located in Stonington, Connecticut, USA.

652.

The property is listed on the National Register of Historic Places and is recognized for its architectural and historical significance.

653.

The Carriagehouse and House were built in the mid-19th century and served as the residence of Austin F. Williams, a successful merchant and banker.

654.

The complex includes the main house, carriagehouse, and surrounding gardens, reflecting the architectural style of the period.

655.

The Italianate architectural style is prevalent in both the main house and the carriagehouse, characterized by ornate details and symmetry.

656.

The Carriagehouse was used to store carriages, horses, and other equipment during the era of horse-drawn transportation.

657.

The property showcases the transition from the agricultural and maritime economy of the 19th century to the industrial era.

658.

The Austin F. Williams House is notable for its well-preserved interior, featuring period furnishings and decor.

659.

The house and carriagehouse have been maintained to reflect the lifestyle of a prosperous 19th-century merchant family.

660.

The property's gardens feature a variety of plant species that were popular during the Victorian era.

661.

The Austin F. Williams Carriagehouse and House provide insights into the social and economic history of the region.

662.

The complex is an example of how historical preservation efforts can bring the past to life for modern audiences.

663.

The house's architecture is a blend of Victorian elements, including ornate woodwork, bay windows, and decorative moldings.

664.

The property's location near the coast is a reminder of the maritime connections that shaped the region's history.

665.

The Carriagehouse served a functional purpose in the 19th century, highlighting the lifestyle and transportation of the time.

666.

The interior of the main house reflects the changing tastes and styles of the Victorian era, from furniture to wallpapers.

667.

The complex has been used for educational programs, tours, and community events that highlight its historical significance.

668.

The gardens surrounding the property showcase plants and landscaping techniques that were popular in the 19th century.

669.

The Austin F. Williams Carriagehouse and House offer visitors a glimpse into the daily life and aspirations of a 19th-century merchant.

670.

The property has been documented in historical records and photographs, providing a rich source of information about its history.

671.

The Carriagehouse and House have been featured in publications and documentaries about Connecticut's architectural heritage.

672.

The complex's preservation efforts demonstrate the importance of maintaining historical landmarks for future generations.

673.

The Austin F. Williams House reflects the influence of architectural trends and societal changes during the Victorian era.

674.

The property's historical interpretation allows visitors to connect with the past and better understand the context of the time.

675.

The Carriagehouse symbolizes the transition from horse-drawn transportation to the rise of automobiles in the 20th century.

676.

The main house's interior showcases intricate woodwork, period furnishings, and decorative features that were popular in the Victorian era.

677.

The Austin F. Williams Carriagehouse and House serve as a reminder of the individuals and families who shaped local history.

678.

The property has been maintained through collaboration between historical organizations, volunteers, and preservationists.

679.

The complex is part of a broader effort to preserve and celebrate Connecticut's architectural and cultural heritage.

680.

The gardens surrounding the property provide a serene and picturesque setting that complements the historical structures.

681.

The Austin F. Williams House stands as a testament to the craftsmanship and attention to detail that defined the Victorian era.

682.

The complex's significance extends beyond its architectural features to its role in the social and economic development of the region.

683.

The Carriagehouse is a tangible link to a bygone era when transportation relied on horses and carriages.

684.

The Austin F. Williams Carriagehouse and House have contributed to the community's sense of identity and historical pride.

685.

The property's guided tours and educational programs offer a deeper understanding of its historical context.

686.

The main house's layout and decor provide a glimpse into the everyday life and routines of the 19th-century occupants.

687.

The Carriagehouse and House are a valuable resource for historians, educators, and anyone interested in local history.

688.

The complex's location in Stonington, a historic maritime town, reflects the connections between land and sea in the region's history.

689.

The gardens surrounding the property showcase a variety of plant species that were cultivated during the Victorian period.

690.

The Austin F. Williams Carriagehouse and House have been recognized for their architectural significance and preservation efforts.

691.

The complex's restoration and maintenance have been guided by historical research and attention to period details.

692.

The main house's architecture reflects the Victorian fascination with ornamentation, symmetry, and aesthetic details.

693.

The Carriagehouse's construction materials and design reflect the practical needs of storing horse-drawn vehicles.

694.

The property's historical interpretation extends to its exterior, interior, and surrounding landscape.

695.

The Austin F. Williams House offers insights into the aspirations, values, and social dynamics of the 19th-century middle class.

696.

The complex's educational programs include tours, workshops, and events that engage visitors with its historical significance.

697.

The Carriagehouse and House have been embraced by the community as a symbol of the region's history and heritage.

698.

The main house's rooms have been restored to reflect the lifestyles and tastes of different family members.

699.

The gardens surrounding the property provide a serene environment for visitors to explore and reflect on the past.

700.

The Austin F. Williams Carriagehouse and House represent a tangible connection to the past, inviting visitors to step back in time and learn about the history of the area.

701.

Hydrozoan jellyfish belong to the class Hydrozoa, a diverse group of marine organisms that include both solitary and colonial species.

702.

Hydrozoans are part of the phylum Cnidaria, which also includes corals, sea anemones, and true jellyfish.

703.

These jellyfish have a complex life cycle that typically includes both a polyp stage and a medusa stage.

704.

The polyp stage of hydrozoan jellyfish resembles a small, tubular organism that attaches to surfaces like rocks or coral reefs.

705.

The medusa stage is what we commonly recognize as a jellyfish, with a bell-shaped body and trailing tentacles.

706.

Hydrozoan jellyfish exhibit a wide range of sizes, from just a few millimeters to several centimeters in diameter.

707.

Some hydrozoan species are bioluminescent, meaning they can emit light, which serves various purposes including attracting prey.

708.

The tentacles of hydrozoan jellyfish are lined with specialized cells called cnidocytes, which contain stinging structures called nematocysts.

709.

Nematocysts are used for both capturing prey and defending against predators by injecting venom.

710.

Different hydrozoan species have varied feeding habits, including filter-feeding, capturing small organisms, and even engaging in symbiotic relationships.

711.

Some species of hydrozoan jellyfish exhibit colonial behavior, forming interconnected groups of polyps that share a common digestive system.

712.

The famous Portuguese Man o' War is not a true jellyfish but a colony of specialized hydrozoan organisms working together.

713.

The lifecycle of hydrozoan jellyfish often involves both sexual and asexual reproduction.

714.

During sexual reproduction, medusae release eggs and sperm into the water, leading to the development of fertilized eggs and eventually new larvae.

715.

Asexual reproduction in hydrozoan jellyfish can occur through budding, where new individuals develop as outgrowths from the parent polyp.

716.

Hydrozoans can be found in various marine environments, from shallow coastal waters to deep ocean habitats.

717.

Some hydrozoan species are known to be bioluminescent, emitting flashes of light in response to disturbances.

718.

Hydrozoans can serve as indicators of environmental health due to their sensitivity to changes in water conditions.

719.

Hydrozoan jellyfish play important roles in marine food webs, both as predators and prey for larger organisms.

720.

They are often preyed upon by various marine animals, including larger jellyfish, sea anemones, and certain fish species.

721.

The study of hydrozoans is essential for understanding the evolution and biodiversity of cnidarians as a whole.

722.

Some hydrozoans exhibit intricate and beautiful patterns in their body structures and tentacle arrangements.

723.

Hydrozoan jellyfish are found in oceans around the world, from the Arctic to the Antarctic.

724.

Some species of hydrozoans are capable of undergoing a process known as transdifferentiation, where one type of cell can transform into another type.

725.

The stinging cells of hydrozoan jellyfish can cause discomfort and skin irritation if they come into contact with humans.

726.

Hydrozoans have been used as model organisms in scientific studies to understand various biological processes.

727.

The genus Hydra is a well-known example of a solitary hydrozoan that is often used in research on regeneration and cell biology.

728.

Certain hydrozoan species are associated with coral reefs and can contribute to the biodiversity and health of these delicate ecosystems.

729.

Hydrozoans are among the oldest living creatures on Earth, with fossil records dating back hundreds of millions of years.

730.

Some hydrozoan species are capable of rapid regeneration, being able to regrow lost parts of their body.

731.

The hydrozoan species Velella velella, also known as "by-the-wind sailors," possesses a sail-like structure that allows it to float on the ocean's surface.

732.

The hydrozoan species Turritopsis dohrnii, also known as the "immortal jellyfish," has the unique ability to revert to its juvenile form after reaching maturity, effectively restarting its life cycle.

733.

Certain hydrozoan species are known to exhibit bioluminescent displays that can be seen as light shows in the open ocean at night.

734.

Hydrozoans are not only found in open water but also in other aquatic environments like freshwater lakes and rivers.

735.

They are often preyed upon by various marine animals, including larger jellyfish, sea anemones, and certain fish species.

736.

Hydrozoans can display a remarkable range of colors and patterns, which may serve as camouflage, attract prey, or deter predators.

737.

Some species of hydrozoans exhibit a symbiotic relationship with photosynthetic organisms like zooxanthellae, providing a mutual benefit.

738.

Hydrozoans can be found at varying depths in the ocean, from the surface to the deep sea.

739.

Some hydrozoan species are considered pests in aquaculture due to their tendency to colonize and damage structures.

740.

The biodiversity of hydrozoan species is still not fully explored, with new discoveries being made as technology and research techniques advance.

741.

Hydrozoan jellyfish have inspired artistic and cultural depictions, appearing in literature, art, and mythology.

742.

Some hydrozoans exhibit a phenomenon called "colony cycling," where medusae are produced in large numbers during specific times of the year.

743.

Hydrozoans are important for scientific studies on regeneration, developmental biology, and even potential medical applications.

744.

The behavior of hydrozoans, such as their movement and feeding patterns, can vary significantly between species.

745.

The tentacles of certain hydrozoan species are covered in specialized cells that emit bioluminescent flashes, possibly to attract prey.

746.

Some hydrozoans have a transparent or translucent appearance, making them difficult to spot in their natural environment.

747.

Hydrozoan jellyfish are often observed in the company of other marine organisms, forming unique ecological relationships.

748.

Some hydrozoans can reproduce rapidly, leading to population blooms that can have ecological and economic impacts.

749.

The study of hydrozoans is vital for understanding the broader marine ecosystem and the interplay between various species.

750.

Overall, hydrozoan jellyfish contribute to the intricate tapestry of marine life, showcasing the fascinating adaptations and relationships that exist within ocean ecosystems.

751.

The Ibisbill (Ibidorhyncha struthersii) is a distinctive bird species found in the mountainous regions of central and southern Asia.

752.

It belongs to its own unique family, Ibidorhynchidae, and is not closely related to other bird families.

753.

The Ibisbill gets its name from its long, down-curved bill, which somewhat resembles that of an ibis.

754.

It is a medium-sized wader bird, with a length of about 40 to 45 cm (15.7 to 17.7 inches) and a wingspan of around 70 to 75 cm (27.5 to 29.5 inches).

755.

Ibisbills have a striking appearance with a white body and black wings, tail, and distinctive facial markings.

756.

The bird's white plumage acts as camouflage against the stony riverbeds and rocky habitats it prefers.

757.

Ibisbills have a unique vocalization, producing a series of musical whistles, trills, and calls that are distinct to their species.

758.

Their calls are often heard during the breeding season as well as when they are foraging along riverbanks.

759.

Ibisbills are found in areas with fast-flowing streams, rivers, and mountainous regions near water bodies.

760.

They are often seen in regions of the Himalayas, such as Bhutan, Nepal, and parts of northern India and China.

761.

Ibisbills are highly territorial during the breeding season, fiercely defending their nesting and foraging areas.

762.

Their diet consists primarily of aquatic insects, small crustaceans, and invertebrates found in the shallow waters of rivers and streams.

763.

Ibisbills have a unique feeding behavior where they use their sensitive bills to probe underwater and detect prey hiding under rocks and debris.

764.

Breeding season for Ibisbills usually occurs during the spring and early summer months.

765.

They build their nests on gravel banks, shingle bars, or small rocky islands along the water's edge.

766.

The nest is a simple scrape in the ground, lined with pebbles, gravel, and vegetation.

767.

Ibisbills lay a clutch of 2 to 3 eggs, which are incubated by both parents for about 22 to 26 days.

768.

Both the male and female take turns incubating the eggs and caring for the chicks.

769.

Ibisbill chicks are precocial, meaning they are born with their eyes open and able to move shortly after hatching.

770.

The young birds are fed by their parents and fledge (develop flight feathers) at around 30 to 40 days.

771.

The IUCN Red List categorizes the Ibisbill as a species of "Least Concern," but its population is believed to be declining due to habitat degradation.

772.

Habitat loss, dam construction, and pollution are some of the threats that impact the Ibisbill's natural habitats.

773.

Due to its elusive behavior and preference for remote habitats, the Ibisbill is not commonly observed by casual birdwatchers.

774.

They are often solitary birds, and pairs are usually only seen together during the breeding season.

775.

The Ibisbill's scientific name, Ibidorhyncha struthersii, honors Dr. Struthers, a Scottish physician and naturalist.

776.

Ibisbills have excellent sight and are capable of detecting movement in the water even from a distance.

777.

The long, curved bill of the Ibisbill allows it to efficiently search for food under stones and crevices.

778.

Despite their wading habits, Ibisbills are strong fliers and can cover considerable distances when needed.

779.

Ibisbills have well-developed and flexible toes that help them grip on slippery rocks and navigate the uneven terrain of their habitats.

780.

They are known to occasionally forage on land for insects, especially during the non-breeding season.

781.

Ibisbills have been observed using their bills to defend themselves from potential predators.

782.

Their wing feathers have a striking iridescence, especially visible in sunlight, which adds to their beauty.

783.

Ibisbills are relatively secretive birds, making them a challenge to observe even for experienced birdwatchers.

784.

They have a unique breeding call that sounds like a soft, melodious whistle.

785.

Ibisbills are well adapted to their cold mountain environments, with dense plumage providing insulation.

786.

The decline in suitable habitats for Ibisbills is a growing concern for their conservation.

787.

Climate change is also affecting the availability of suitable breeding and foraging habitats for these birds.

788.

Their unique appearance and habits make them a target for bird enthusiasts seeking to add a rare and intriguing species to their list.

789.

The Ibisbill's long bill and probing behavior are adaptations that allow them to exploit food sources that other birds might miss.

790.

The Ibisbill's black facial markings and eye patches contrast strikingly against its white plumage.

791.

Ibisbills are not migratory birds, and they tend to remain in their breeding and foraging areas throughout the year.

792.

In some regions, Ibisbills are considered symbolic and hold cultural significance.

793.

The intricate patterns of their plumage make them challenging to spot in their natural habitats.

794.

Ibisbills have relatively short legs, which are well-suited for moving along rocky riverbeds.

795.

Their long bills are adapted for precision, allowing them to catch small and elusive prey.

796.

The call of the Ibisbill is often described as melodious and pleasant, adding to its allure for bird enthusiasts.

797.

Ibisbills are known to have a low reproductive rate, which makes them vulnerable to population declines.

798.

Their elusive nature and remote habitats contribute to limited scientific knowledge about their behaviors and habits.

799.

The Ibisbill's habitat preference for rocky, fast-flowing rivers and streams makes it difficult to study and monitor.

800.

The conservation of Ibisbills requires collaborative efforts to protect their habitats, raise awareness, and promote sustainable practices that benefit both these unique birds and the ecosystems they inhabit.

801.

Atlassian was founded in 2002 by Mike Cannon-Brookes and Scott Farquhar in Sydney, Australia.

802.

The company's name "Atlassian" is a combination of "Atlas," representing strength and reliability, and "Marathon," representing endurance and dedication.

803.

Atlassian's first product was JIRA, a software application initially designed for bug and issue tracking.

804.

The founders started Atlassian with a $10,000 credit card debt and no outside funding.

805.

Atlassian's success story began when they created a software product for themselves to track and manage their own projects.

806.

Their initial goal was to make a product that was simple to use yet powerful for software development teams.

807.

JIRA's success led to the formation of Atlassian as a company, as they realized the potential to help other teams with similar challenges.

808.

Atlassian's unique approach of providing software tools that help teams work more efficiently became their guiding philosophy.

809.

The company's first office was located above a garage in Sydney, Australia.

810.

Confluence, Atlassian's second major product, was launched in 2004. It is a collaboration and content management tool.

811.

Atlassian's open company culture encourages transparency, collaboration, and trust among employees.

812.

In 2006, Atlassian expanded its international presence by opening an office in San Francisco, USA.

813.

Atlassian became a publicly traded company in 2015 when it debuted on the NASDAQ stock exchange under the symbol "TEAM."

814.

The company has a unique tradition of releasing an April Fools' Day product every year, ranging from quirky tools to innovative ideas.

815.

Atlassian's products are widely used across various industries, including technology, finance, healthcare, and more.

816.

Trello, a popular project management tool, was acquired by Atlassian in 2017, expanding its product portfolio.

817.

Atlassian's products are known for their flexibility and the ability to be customized to fit specific team workflows.

818.

The company introduced the "Team Playbook," a collection of free tools and practices designed to help teams work better together.

819.

Atlassian's core values, known as "SHIP," stand for "Selfless," "Human," "Innovative," and "Play, as a team."

820.

The founders have remained actively involved in the company's operations and have been recognized as influential figures in the tech industry.

821.

Atlassian's mission is to unleash the potential of every team, enabling them to collaborate, create, and innovate more effectively.

822.

The company's revenue model is based on a subscription-based SaaS (Software as a Service) model.

823.

Atlassian's products are used by organizations of all sizes, from startups to multinational corporations.

824.

The company has a strong commitment to social responsibility and contributes to various charitable initiatives.

825.

Atlassian's annual conference, "Atlassian Summit," brings together users, partners, and enthusiasts from around the world to share insights and knowledge.

826.

In 2019, Atlassian introduced a free cloud version of its flagship product, JIRA Software, to make it more accessible to smaller teams.

827.

Atlassian emphasizes the importance of diversity and inclusion and is committed to building a more diverse workforce.

828.

The company offers a wide range of certifications for its products, helping professionals enhance their skills and expertise.

829.

Atlassian's founders are known for their philanthropic efforts, including investments in education, technology, and environmental conservation.

830.

The company often shares its experiences and learnings through its blogs, webinars, and resources, contributing to the larger tech community.

831.

In 2021, Atlassian announced a major strategic partnership with Slack to improve integrations between their respective products.

832.

Atlassian has a unique approach to performance reviews, where employees set their own goals and review each other's contributions.

833.

The company has received numerous awards and recognitions for its workplace culture and commitment to employee well-being.

834.

Atlassian encourages a healthy work-life balance, offering flexible work arrangements and promoting employee mental health.

835.

Bitbucket, another product by Atlassian, is a Git repository management solution that helps teams collaborate on code development.

836.

Atlassian encourages hackathons and innovation challenges to foster creativity among its employees.

837.

The company's commitment to agile development principles is reflected in its product development processes.

838.

In 2020, Atlassian acquired Mindville, a Swedish company that specializes in asset and configuration management solutions.

839.

Atlassian maintains a strong commitment to security, ensuring that its products adhere to the highest industry standards.

840.

The company's unique mascot, the "Atlasian," is often seen in various forms across their branding and events.

841.

Atlassian's community includes a wide range of users, including software developers, project managers, content creators, and more.

842.

The Atlassian Marketplace offers a plethora of third-party apps and integrations that enhance the functionality of Atlassian products.

843.

Atlassian's headquarters in Sydney is designed with an open and collaborative workspace to encourage interaction among employees.

844.

The company frequently hosts "ShipIt Days," where employees have the opportunity to work on innovative projects outside their usual responsibilities.

845.

Atlassian Foundation, the company's charitable arm, supports various initiatives focused on education and social impact.

846.

Atlassian's "Team Tour" events bring thought leaders, experts, and practitioners together to discuss best practices in teamwork.

847.

The company's commitment to sustainability is evident in its efforts to reduce its carbon footprint and promote eco-friendly practices.

848.

Atlassian's values extend to its partners and customers, fostering a sense of community and collaboration.

849.

The company's commitment to continuous improvement is reflected in its frequent product updates and new feature releases.

850.

Atlassian's history is marked by a relentless pursuit of innovation, a dedication to helping teams succeed, and a strong sense of social responsibility that continues to shape its path forward.

851.

Bristol Myers Squibb (BMS) was founded in 1887 by William McLaren Bristol and John Ripley Myers in Clinton, New York.

852.

The company's first product was a mineral-based medicine called "Sal Hepatica," used to treat digestive disorders.

853.

In the early 20th century, BMS introduced a line of pharmaceuticals, including products for pain relief, colds, and skin conditions.

854.

The company's research efforts in the 1930s led to the development of a pioneering anticoagulant drug, dicoumarol.

855.

BMS played a significant role during World War II by producing penicillin for the U.S. military.

856.

In 1959, Bristol Myers became one of the first pharmaceutical companies to launch a comprehensive advertising campaign to promote its products.

857.

The merger of Bristol Myers and Squibb Corporation took place in 1989, forming Bristol Myers Squibb.

858.

The merger allowed the company to expand its product portfolio and research capabilities significantly.

859.

Bristol Myers Squibb has a strong focus on oncology, cardiovascular disease, and immunology research.

860.

The company introduced Plavix (clopidogrel), a blockbuster antiplatelet drug, in the late 1990s.

861.

In 2002, BMS and Sanofi-Aventis jointly launched Plavix, becoming one of the most prescribed medications globally.

862.

The company's efforts in HIV/AIDS research led to the development of Reyataz (atazanavir), an important treatment for the disease.

863.

Bristol Myers Squibb's immunotherapy drug, Opdivo (nivolumab), was approved for the treatment of certain cancers, revolutionizing cancer care.

864.

The acquisition of Celgene Corporation in 2019 marked one of the largest biopharmaceutical deals in history, expanding BMS's pipeline.

865.

Bristol Myers Squibb's commitment to patient advocacy is evident through initiatives like "Patient Voice Impact Awards" and "Ready. Raise. Rise."

866.

The company's corporate citizenship programs focus on supporting global health, education, and community initiatives.

867.

BMS has received recognition for its commitment to diversity and inclusion, including being named to the Bloomberg Gender-Equality Index.

868.

The company's core values include a dedication to innovation, patient-centricity, accountability, integrity, and teamwork.

869.

Bristol Myers Squibb's headquarters is located in New York City, and it has operations in various countries worldwide.

870.

The company's commitment to scientific discovery is exemplified by its investment in research and development.

871.

BMS's efforts in drug development extend to rare diseases, with breakthrough treatments for conditions like hereditary angioedema.

872.

The "Bristol Myers Squibb Foundation" supports various health equity and social justice initiatives globally.

873.

The company's portfolio includes both prescription medicines and over-the-counter products.

874.

Bristol Myers Squibb invests in early-stage research through collaborations with academia and startup companies.

875.

The company has a strong focus on innovative partnerships to advance drug discovery and development.

876.

BMS's "Patient Access Support" programs aim to make its medicines more accessible to patients in need.

877.

The company's involvement in clinical trials allows patients to access investigational treatments and contribute to medical advancement.

878.

Bristol Myers Squibb has been recognized for its efforts to reduce its environmental impact and promote sustainable practices.

879.

The company's collaborations with patient advocacy organizations aim to raise awareness and address unmet medical needs.

880.

BMS's commitment to scientific excellence is reflected in its research awards, scholarships, and grants for emerging scientists.

881.

Bristol Myers Squibb's global presence allows it to reach patients in diverse communities and healthcare systems.

882.

The company's investment in digital health and technology has led to innovative patient-centric solutions.

883.

BMS's therapeutic expertise encompasses a wide range of medical conditions, including cardiovascular diseases, neurological disorders, and more.

884.

The company's commitment to safety is reflected in its comprehensive pharmacovigilance and risk management programs.

885.

Bristol Myers Squibb supports healthcare professionals through medical education programs and resources.

886.

The company's pipeline includes potential treatments for diseases with significant unmet medical needs.

887.

BMS's efforts in research extend to novel approaches like gene therapy and precision medicine.

888.

The acquisition of MyoKardia in 2020 added potential transformative therapies for cardiovascular diseases to the company's portfolio.

889.

Bristol Myers Squibb's contributions to global health include partnerships to fight infectious diseases like tuberculosis and hepatitis.

890.

The company's "OneBMS" initiative fosters collaboration and synergy across diverse teams and disciplines.

891.

Bristol Myers Squibb is committed to ethical business practices and compliance with all applicable laws and regulations.

892.

The company's "Bristol Myers Squibb Employee Giving Program" supports charitable organizations chosen by employees.

893.

BMS's commitment to sustainability is evident in its efforts to reduce waste, water usage, and greenhouse gas emissions.

894.

The company's financial stability allows it to invest in groundbreaking research and development.

895.

Bristol Myers Squibb's "Together with Patients" initiative underscores its dedication to putting patients at the center of everything it does.

896.

The company's collaborations with academic institutions and research centers help advance medical science.

897.

BMS's focus on cell therapy research has the potential to revolutionize the treatment of various diseases.

898.

Bristol Myers Squibb's philanthropic efforts include supporting disaster relief and humanitarian aid globally.

899.

The company's expansion into emerging markets allows it to address healthcare challenges in underserved areas.

900.

Bristol Myers Squibb's legacy of innovation, patient-centered care, and dedication to scientific advancement continues to shape its impact on global health.

901.

The William Williams House is a historic home located in Lebanon, Connecticut, USA.

902.

The house was built in 1751 by William Williams, a signer of the Declaration of Independence.

903.

William Williams was a delegate to the Continental Congress and played a significant role in American independence.

904.

The house is an example of Georgian architecture and reflects the colonial style of the mid-18th century.

905.

The William Williams House is one of the best-preserved colonial-era homes in Connecticut.

906.

The house has a central chimney, a symmetrical façade, and traditional woodwork.

907.

William Williams used the house as his residence and law office.

908.

The house remained in the Williams family for several generations.

909.

The William Williams House is designated as a National Historic Landmark.

910.

The house is now operated as a museum and is open to the public.

911.

Visitors can explore the well-preserved rooms and learn about the life of William Williams and his contributions to American history.

912.

The house contains original period furniture, artifacts, and documents.

913.

The William Williams House showcases the lifestyle of a colonial-era family, providing insights into daily life during that time.

914.

The property features beautiful gardens and landscaping that reflect the aesthetics of the 18th century.

915.

The house has been carefully restored to maintain its historical accuracy and authenticity.

916.

The William Williams House is a popular destination for history enthusiasts and school groups.

917.

The house serves as a reminder of the individuals who played crucial roles in shaping the nation's history.

918.

The property offers guided tours that delve into the history of the house, the Williams family, and the American Revolution.

919.

The house often hosts special events, lectures, and educational programs related to colonial history.

920.

The preservation of the William Williams House is a testament to the importance of honoring the founding fathers and their legacies.

921.

The house provides a glimpse into the challenges and achievements of early American settlers.

922.

The William Williams House is located in a picturesque setting that captures the essence of colonial New England.

923.

The property has been documented as an essential part of Connecticut's architectural heritage.

924.

The architecture of the house reflects the craftsmanship and design principles of its time.

925.

The William Williams House contributes to the cultural heritage of Lebanon and the state of Connecticut.

926.

The house is a symbol of the enduring impact of individuals who played a role in the fight for American independence.

927.

The house's historical significance extends beyond its physical structure, encompassing the stories and values of its inhabitants.

928.

Preservation efforts ensure that future generations can appreciate and learn from the history represented by the William Williams House.

929.

The house is often featured in historical tours and programs that highlight Connecticut's role in the American Revolution.

930.

The William Williams House is a destination for those interested in exploring early American architecture and history.

931.

The property offers an immersive experience that transports visitors back in time to colonial Connecticut.

932.

The museum staff provides insights into the restoration process and the challenges of preserving historical buildings.

933.

The William Williams House is part of the Connecticut Freedom Trail, a network of sites associated with the state's African American history and the fight for civil rights.

934.

The house's architecture incorporates elements that reflect the values and ideals of the colonial era.

935.

The house stands as a testament to the perseverance and dedication of preservationists who have ensured its survival.

936.

The William Williams House captures the essence of a significant period in American history when the nation was being born.

937.

The property offers a serene and contemplative atmosphere that allows visitors to connect with the past.

938.

The William Williams House serves as a reminder that historic preservation contributes to a deeper understanding of cultural heritage.

939.

The house's location in a rural setting provides insights into early American agrarian lifestyles.

940.

The museum offers educational programs that engage visitors of all ages with interactive and immersive experiences.

941.

The William Williams House is an important resource for scholars researching colonial history and the lives of prominent figures.

942.

The preservation of the house honors William Williams and his contributions to the founding of the United States.

943.

The property's gardens showcase plants and landscaping techniques that were common during the colonial era.

944.

The museum's exhibits explore the political climate of the 18th century and the challenges faced by early American patriots.

945.

The William Williams House provides an opportunity to explore the cultural and social context of colonial New England.

946.

The house is an anchor for heritage tourism and contributes to the local economy by attracting visitors to the region.

947.

The property's connection to William Williams links visitors directly to a signer of one of America's most important documents.

948.

The William Williams House serves as an inspiration for other preservation projects and community initiatives.

949.

The museum's programming encourages visitors to reflect on the values of liberty and democracy that shaped the nation.

950.

The William Williams House continues to play a vital role in preserving and sharing the stories of America's past for present and future generations.

951.

The Oliver Wolcott House is a historic home located in Litchfield, Connecticut, USA.

952.

The house was built in 1753 by Oliver Wolcott Sr., a signer of the Declaration of Independence.

953.

Oliver Wolcott Sr. was also a distinguished military officer and served as a governor of Connecticut.

954.

The house is a fine example of Georgian architecture, characterized by its symmetry and elegant design.

955.

The Oliver Wolcott House is a two-story, wood-framed structure with a central chimney.

956.

The house has a symmetrical façade with evenly spaced windows and a centrally located entrance.

957.

The interior of the house features period-specific details, including decorative woodwork and furnishings.

958.

Oliver Wolcott Sr. used the house as his residence, where he lived with his wife and family.

959.

The house remained in the Wolcott family for several generations and was a center of political and social activity.

960.

The Oliver Wolcott House is designated as a National Historic Landmark.

961.

The house has been carefully preserved and restored to showcase its original 18th-century charm.

962.

Visitors to the house can explore the rooms, furnishings, and artifacts that provide insights into colonial life.

963.

The house offers guided tours that delve into the history of the Wolcott family and their contributions to American history.

964.

The Oliver Wolcott House serves as a testament to Oliver Wolcott Sr.'s commitment to the American Revolution.

965.

The property is a representation of the lifestyle of a prominent colonial-era family.

966.

The house's architecture reflects the wealth and status of its occupants during the 18th century.

967.

The gardens and landscaping around the house mirror the aesthetics of the time and provide a peaceful atmosphere.

968.

The Oliver Wolcott House provides a connection to the founding of the United States and the ideals of liberty.

969.

The house is a prime example of how historic homes can serve as educational resources and cultural treasures.

970.

The property often hosts events, workshops, and educational programs related to colonial history.

971.

Preservation efforts have ensured that the house remains a valuable resource for scholars and visitors alike.

972.

The Oliver Wolcott House offers a glimpse into the challenges and successes of early American patriots.

973.

The house's location in Litchfield, known for its historical significance, enhances its cultural context.

974.

The architecture and design of the Oliver Wolcott House reflect the refined tastes of the colonial elite.

975.

The property showcases the craftsmanship and attention to detail that were characteristic of the period.

976.

The Oliver Wolcott House is an important part of Litchfield's historical and architectural heritage.

977.

The house is recognized as a site of national importance due to its connection to the American Revolution.

978.

Preservation organizations and volunteers have played a vital role in maintaining and interpreting the house.

979.

The museum staff provides informative tours that offer insights into the daily lives of the Wolcott family.

980.

The Oliver Wolcott House serves as an inspiration for those interested in preserving historical homes.

981.

The property contributes to the understanding of how families of the colonial era lived and interacted.

982.

The house is a testament to the impact of individuals who played roles in shaping the nation's early history.

983.

The Oliver Wolcott House provides an authentic representation of a colonial New England home.

984.

The museum's exhibits offer perspectives on Oliver Wolcott Sr.'s role in both state and national politics.

985.

The house is situated in a serene environment that transports visitors back to a bygone era.

986.

The Oliver Wolcott House is a source of pride for the local community and the state of Connecticut.

987.

The house's significance extends beyond its architecture, encompassing the stories of the Wolcott family.

988.

Visitors can learn about the challenges faced by colonial families and the decisions they made during a pivotal period.

989.

The Oliver Wolcott House is often visited by students, history enthusiasts, and those interested in genealogy.

990.

The preservation of the house honors the legacy of Oliver Wolcott Sr. and his contributions to the nation's birth.

991.

The house's design reflects the influence of English architectural styles prevalent during the colonial period.

992.

The property offers opportunities for visitors to engage with history through interactive displays and programs.

993.

The Oliver Wolcott House showcases the role of individuals who worked tirelessly to secure American independence.

994.

The museum's educational initiatives encourage visitors to reflect on the principles of democracy and freedom.

995.

The house's architecture is a blend of practicality and elegance, reflective of colonial lifestyles.

996.

The Oliver Wolcott House's interpretation emphasizes the local and national importance of its occupants.

997.

The house is part of a network of historic sites that collectively tell the story of early American history.

998.

The preservation of the house contributes to the ongoing dialogue about America's founding ideals.

999.

The Oliver Wolcott House serves as a reminder of the sacrifices made by those who fought for liberty.

1000.

The property's role as a historic site highlights the value of preserving tangible connections to the past for future generations.

www.ingramcontent.com/pod-product-compliance
Lightning Source LLC
Chambersburg PA
CBHW070805260726
48660CB00005B/1718